A S[illegible]ty Prolonged

Chenson A. Bennett

Tamarind Hill Press
www.tamarindhillpress.co.uk
First published in 2020

A Sinner's Insanity Prolonged

London, United Kingdom

ISBN

978-1-64786-429-3

TAMARiND HiLL .PRESS

BOOK REVIEWS

Chenson Bennett's *A Sinner's Insanity Prolonged* is a captivating poetry collection concerning love, self-worth, and spirituality. The collection of poems is intimate and personal. Each poem prioritizes developing meaning, taking a brief plunge into its themes, which are suggested by the titles. They include beautiful lines of appealing imagery. For example:

"The first kiss, I felt you tremble;
the first touch, I heard you moan."

Verses are centered on the page, grounding them in their core themes. The tactic is sometimes a graceful touch, as with the short poem "Angel in a Human Body":

"She's like an angel, her dark skin so pure.
A fizzle in my mind, I'm so confused; this line is confusing."

These reminders of an individuals' inner beauty and divinity are encouraging. Even more powerful is the simile which relates the woman to an "angel": pure, valuable, and desired.

The word choices are emotive and powerful with metaphors used to portray experiences in a suggestive way. The language is straightforward, capturing the deep and intense issues being addressed. The tone is consistent and so is the narrative. The poems appeal to the senses.
A recurring theme is love framing these poems in a wider manner. Enlivening the poems and providing a deeper meaning.

—Saun-Jaye Brown author of Consciously 21

§

"I was the shadow in the shadows" is the epitome of his style. These words jumped from the pages and attacked every fibre of my soul. As I read each piece, I was drawn in by the words that became life on the pages "written with his blood."
Amazing, brilliant, creative, abstraction at its core used to create life on pages which has left my mind perpetually stained with images; pictures painted that will last a lifetime. Drawing on spirituality, Chenson pulls on the emotions of the soul; using the reality of one's experience to capture the imagination. A must read for the lover of poetry, Chenson Bennett has produced a masterpiece of simplistic complexity, poetry for the contemporary,

poetry we can relate to. Fingers snapping for you Chenson!

–Antonio J. Erskine author of <u>The Truth of Emotions</u>

§

This book is definitely one of the most intriguing short poetry books I've ever read. I'm very excited to see it publish to get a copy and start sharing quotes from it on social media. Line after line, it got me wanting to read more. The author has a very unique way of capturing the reader's imagination.

— **F. Stabbs**

§

Beautifully written collection of poems that addresses an array of complex and intense emotions that practically everyone can relate to - love, lust, greed, grief, guilt and pride to name a few. I thoroughly enjoyed the raw outpouring of emotions as the poet tries to make sense of his experiences and the world around him.

–Suwan Satahoo

ACKNOWLEDGEMENTS

To the children of thought, this book has been written as a dedication to you.

To the children of pain, I hope these words soothe your wounds and refresh your heart.

To the children who linger in this world, I hope you find your root in these pages.

ABOUT THE POET

I am a spring
which rose from the earth,
who developed into a river
and paved my path,
making my way to the sea
which is in the ocean
connecting endlessly.
Here, I can achieve all my desires.

I am nothing
but something,
nor someone,
who sees these patterns
and realizes that everything is nothing,
and nothing is everything.
The lies we believe
is the faith we cling to
and the *gods* we serve is everything.
So I,

when I question it, is
nothing but a wandering, wondering, soul.

—
Chenson Bennett

Table of Contents

A THOUGHT

You breathe a bit of life as you admire it. Something about it makes it so beautiful—it is incomplete. There's this flux claim about the beauty of perfection—I don't see it—because, when perfection is achieved, what is left for the dreamer, the scientist and the philosopher?

A piece of art, it's at its most, when it is drawn by the dying artist, because, when he expires, and the art is at its near completion, he gives his all; he gives his artistic nakedness to the mind and exposes the mind to something cognitively ecstatic... Imagine an art that evolves as your intellectual space terraforms—this, in the beauty of the incomplete art piece, is perfection.

Eternally Thinking

The world—a mass of creativity—a mass of
imbalanced creativity,
compressed into a perfect symphony,
divided between perfection and corruption.
It's hard to tell the true separation.

I am left thinking. . .

To what extent is corruption built into the
human consciousness?
To what extent does greed fuel our thirst,
and will that forever allow us to be thirsty?
What is the price we put on life and does
one life equal another; or does one life has
a higher price?
Also, how is it our destruction is seen as
advancement?

I am left thinking. . .

Does one's heart, emotions and feelings
mean nothing?
Does selfishness run so deep in us that we
don't even love our own life?
Does hatred build us, or does it kill us
spiritually?
Yet why is it that sympathy is given to ones
who least deserve it?

I am left thinking. . .

We kill to survive, yet look what killing has
done to the loved ones of the ones killed.
Our course of action is mostly violence!
If we're the most intelligent beings, why do
we revert to animalistic behaviours?
Why do we lie to the young to "protect"
them?
Why do we hate what we can't
understand?

I am left thinking. . .

Would the world be better without us?

Would it be perfect?
Can every question be answered perfectly?
Will we eternally be at war with ourselves?

These questions...

I am left thinking, I am eternally thinking.
Because the mind is an eternal spectrum,
which generates questions and boasts
answers.
So, one day, someday, we may have an
answer.

A Sinner's Tears

A Sinner's Tears

Forgive me, Father, for I have sinned.
I've been rejected by my own heart.
My angels strayed and now I'm in my own darkness.
Forgive me Father as I look to the heavens and call out your name.
My intoxications have consumed me,
and my mind is now opened.
I have been a fool; I now reap corrupted plants—
I sew no righteous seeds.

Forgive me, oh Father,
and allow your angels to touch me once more;
touch me personally and wash my temple white,
wipe these tears from my eyes
and truly open them once more.
For, I have coveted my neighbor with my lust for too long.

Wash my tongue Father,
For I have spoken lies—
I have become a spiritual criminal for
worldly satisfaction,
and little did I know that
I was sentenced to death.

But Father you are my judge.
As I look to the heavens,
I ask for your forgiveness—
to give me the strength once more,
to face these challenges and start a new
page.

Act One

"Thou shall not have any gods before me,"
he said.
As I rest my head,
I praise myself.
I lived in a dream of blood and snow.
How could you believe in a spirit when life
is so alluring?

Intoxication–
a darkened soul
drenched in a sinner's sweat.
Life pulled me in its honey.
Sin was sweet.

...

I was the bee making the honey;
stinging at the angels.
Blackening the wings on my shoulders,
my guardians departed from me,
my tempters drew closer.

My angels watched from afar,

the *idols*–they stepped from the dark.
They came on my level;
I became one also.
I was the shadow in the shadows, but
now in the mirror,
I saw myself higher than a human.

Act Two

"You shall not make for yourself a carved image or any likeness of anything that is in heaven above, or that is in the earth beneath, or that is in the water under the earth."

I worshiped myself; I washed my face in my spiritual crimes,
envied by most, loved by many.
Forgive them, Father, if you can hear, for I do not forgive.
I was higher, much more refined.
I idolized myself.
I believed I was great.
I achieved my works.
I achieved my status. I am far above these infidels.
In the mirror, I am a god.
How can I believe in you when I have myself?

This blasphemous mentality has grown on me.

I walked alone in these gutters for too long.
I swept the feet of others,
and now I am at the top.

Now I am an idol,
and I will not release this throne.

Act Three

"Thou shalt not take the name of the Lord
thy God in vain."

Jesus Christ,
the world is a failure.
The depth of pain grows on my heart more
and more.
I have realized the truth is a burden;
The lies are the *light,*
and the flesh is temporary, but the *memory*
is permanent.

I have realized that words are free; life is
priced.

I have seen that the tree of life branches off
in many corners,
and I have chosen this branch.

When I look up, I only see a blank sky;
I only see empty streets.

Jesus, why have you forsaken me like the rest?
Is it because I want to be like a god?
Jesus!
Is this my punishment?
To live in sin.

Act Four

"Remember the sabbath day, to keep it holy."

No,
every day is a party;
my transgressions are my home.
All these music, drugs and liquor intoxicate my soul.
When I stumble home at nights and when I cough up blood,
I remember that I'm destroying the past.
Because I remember nothing,
I repeat the process again.
I guess I'll never learn.
I have no regrets, no regrets at all.
If all I have to do in life is this,
it would be heaven on earth.
Party all night; vomit all day.
Holiness has no resemblance to play.

Act Five

"Honor thy father and thy mother: that thy days may be long."

Father, Mother, where are you
when I wanted you to hold me close?
Where were you when you should have
offered me advice?
How can I honor you when I lived in
solitude?

Were you there when I spoke to the walls,
when my conscience spoke to me and
drove me to
insanity?
Where were your whispers to soothe?

When I went in the wrong direction?
You circled your own desires like vultures,
and when I was in the middle and the *right*
was so far,
I was pulled into the quicksand.

Now, I was deserted and my heart is
empty.
I fill it with self-righteousness and gluttony.
No father's love.
No mother's love.
No parental teachings.
I am on my own—so relentless, and chaos
is
my teacher.
At the bottom of this quicksand
will be my body waiting to be buried.

Act Six

"Thou shalt not kill."

Mercy is given to the weak;
death is a bliss of enchantment,.
"Thou shalt not kill," the father bestowed upon us,
but the blood already stained the ground.

One blow to the chest.
For a moment, my heart became cold,
my blood became heated,
my sweat wash my skin cold–
and you were dead.
Never have I felt such a craving for murder.
My brother, you have forsaken me like the rest,
and like the rest you should go.
But your existence will be removed,
and now brother, I'll sever the bond,
before your body hits the ground.

I remember your betrayal,
and you'll be dead.

Act Seven

"Thou shalt not commit adultery."

"Find my weak spot and let's fuck till the sun rises."

She's a freak, she's a demon,
she's a witch—but I like her.
She bites my neck.
She tears my flesh.
She bites her lips and she begs for more.
Our bodies get heated;
a room filled with heavy breathing.
She calls my name.
I guess I'm achieving.
We're not friends but this is our hello;
this is our goodbye.
Fuck till the day lights;
fuck to fill the lust.
This is no romance—just a touch of the G-spot,
just a pinch of the nipple,
and caressing of the body,

a tremble of faith,
a vibration of pain,
and moaning of satisfaction.
She turns around slowly and take it deep
inside.
Damn, I love this chick.
She screams my name,
and cools her body with a blushed cum.
Then I cum, and her day is lit.

Act Eight

"Thou shalt not steal."

In a garden of roses,
run away far,
bask in the pollen-filled air,
breathe in its refreshing fill.
Lay down in the garden and open your heart.
Let me steal your property
and run away far.

All the lies, I drilled in your head:
all my words meant nothing.
It was just a test to see how foolish you are.
I stole your heart.
Now I will use it against your mind.

Now lay on this table pure virgin,
and let me paint thy wool black.
Let's sacrifice your purity.
Let's turn your life over on a new page.

Let's fill thy heart to its full content.
Let your true human nature take its course.

Let me steal your heart
and covet thy mind.

Act Nine

"Thou shalt not bear false witness against thy neighbor."

The cold sting against my ears; the heated
betrayal you whisper.
You sound so convincing when you look
me in my eyes; you sound so innocent.
Your words weaken me but your lies
strengthen me.
The smile of the deceitful fades as you turn
away;
that second face you have just been taken
off display.
Have you gone to brainwash another, to
harden the heart of another
with one colder sting?

To inspire the growth of fed lies that
bloom into black roses?
But here's a turn of events:
when you walk into the Garden of Eden
and the tranquility palms its face,

your lies turn the venom that strengthens
the serpent.

It finds you, it coils you, and it bites you.
Your lies poison you.
Now your body feels numb. Ah yes, I
know it does.
They say you reap the seeds you sow; now
you feel the lies as you lie in the constrict
of your reformation of betrayal.

Now you die from your lies.

Act Ten
"The Final Act"

" You shall not covet your neighbor's house. You shall not covet your neighbor's wife."

Though I see myself as being higher,
there is something missing -
your cocky smile, your stream of
happiness.
What do you have over me?

Such a beautiful wife, such a happy
household.
What's missing from my life?
Is what I am living a lie?
Is my life empty?

All these writing on my heart blocks this
spiritual connection.
What you have—why can't I attain it?
This black spiraling cloud surrounds me;
I am greatly misguided.

I don’t know which light to use to guide my way,
and your happiness mocks me.
What do you have?

Why is your *household* so perfect?

I want what you have.
I covet your success.
I covet the fact that you have *experienced*...

Moving On

When a heart is broken once, it rebuilds
itself with hardened steel.
When a bone is crushed, give the body
time—it will move again;
this is life.
A road, scattered with debris,
pale,
bleak,
empty,
because you must walk your own path.
When your heart is shattered,
and a door slams in your face,
stop—wait, and open it again.
That's just one bad experience.

Ten miles of a wide-open road—

This is life.
Enjoy the scenery; keep moving.

Black skies which are filled with lightning,

Several claps of thunder and scarring
memories.

This is life.
Keep moving.

Wide seas, covered in mysteries and its
lure,
it drags you down and spits you up.
When you're lost,
what will you do?

Tears wash your face, fear floods your
mind.
Pace your life; live it.
Fear is true, but know that it allows you to
live.
You only live once.
Keep moving.

The Change

They thanked their gods, looking down on
me when I was in the bitter of the world.
But it's ordinary—being exiled and beaten,
walked over like a dog.
I guess the dirt was my only friend because
it stuck to me to the end—it was the only
thing that rubbed my cheek when I was
down.
But that's an imagery people would say,
"Were you there when I was knocked off
my feet?"

No!
So, shut the hell up!

Sometimes when they look at me, I feel as
if gravity is crushing my lungs.
God answers prayers, *so I guess that is why
I am not dead as yet.* But when they speak,
I feel the sting of their tongues.

Sometimes I'm so lonely, so scared, and
afraid of the world.
I try to get out by playing a game of
Russian roulette, just to make it out,
1 click
2 click
3 click
I couldn't go for four.
No, no more. Its time, time for a change.
Too much.
There is too much to do, too much I
haven't accomplished.
He's a change. I'm strong, the gods are
nothing but servants of their own disgrace
whom they force upon the less fortunate,
so the mask I now have will be torn off—
The last tear—
the new face, the ultimate change.

Love You to Death in Autumn

The leaves burnt red and their hearts
turned yellow.
Where has the love gone? The words they
speak are bullets to each other.
The darkness of their love is only
measurable by the blistering midnight
winds which torture their shells,
stripping them and tearing the leaves from
them—one by one.

This was love; they held each other, such a
dark love.
This is love; they whispered to each other.
With a cold blade, they slit each other.
This love is strong—
What a miserable love.

They kissed the poison off each other's lips
and dined on the
lust they had for each other.

Ahh, the breeze brushed past their faces
and the dead leaves pushed through their
love.
The sweet, sweet, smell of love; they fell to
their knees.
Their wrists bled–the leaves pushed–and
in each other's eyes they looked–
One last kiss, before they plunged
and signed the deal,
for in the eyes of death, they looked.
The heat was strong yet the breeze which
brushed them was so cold.
Their lips part and a shock struck in each–
a cold blade to the chest was each lover's
end.

Last Cry Part 2—I Loved You Too

I saw you, and yes, I heard your heavy words, your face grim with pain; I can hear it.
My heart took its last pound, but I could remember a sweet face on a shy guy, warm tears boiling with sorrow-beating with regret-calling out my name.
I'm flushed. I'm trying to smile too, but my body is feeling cold. I wish I could hold your hands;
it was a satisfaction beyond the warmest sensation on the most frigid of days.
Oh God—I can't believe I'm moving on.
Can the dead even cry? Because I feel like I'm bleeding through my eyes.
The sugar-sweet memories of our childhood; I've watched you grow, now the memories of the past are just fading away.

Darling, darling, please stop crying. I know how you feel.

Death is unavoidable; it was just my time.
I guess God was ready.
But it is sweet knowing that I knew you,
that makes this death so sweet.
From the white roses you placed at my
door in the dark,
never knowing that I prefer the red ones,
but I thought it funny how you still brought
them.
But when I heard you call me angel,
I knew why you chose the whites.
On my last breath, I would whisper in your
ears that it was great knowing you—that shy,
young man.
We're both to blame; we read each other's
mind, but we wasted time.
Still you know that I loved you too,
Even in Heaven or Hell, I'll always
remember you.

The Ugly Truth
(A girl's Silent Fantasy)

You looked at me, the scream was in your
eyes before I actually heard it from your
mouth.
The pitter-patter, the drips, the drop of
warm blood coursed from my hands.
It wasn't me, I wanted to say, but your face
silenced me.
Your horror shook my body; I didn't want
to see you like this.
Please don't be afraid. I tried to reach out,
but I couldn't, my guilt was too much.
You finally screamed, the night got colder
when your voice chilled the air.
Don't be afraid. He died quickly; the knife
in his chest ended it fast.
His blood is getting cold, his heart stopped
minutes ago.
You see these tears on my face? I was
crying too.

You see my clothes? Torn and bloody—
right—we were fighting.
I guess you want to kill me too, right,
Mom?
You wouldn't understand; this man lying
here was wicked.
You moved towards me. Do you want to
force your hand in my face like him?
Or do you want to plunge the knife in my
chest?
Your husband was wicked; he didn't love
you, Mom.
"*Why*?" you ask. You can't manage the
truth,
but I'll tell you because he valued me
more. I had to kill him.
"Your husband tried to rape me!"

The Final Moments

The television fired, breaking news hits the
air, chaos and screams rain on the peak of
the highest mountain.
Everyone valued their lives; *this is the end?*
The rich rushed to safety; was your money
all worth it?
You all used the poor as foot mats; now
you're clustering with them, begging,
pleading with them.
Mother Nature is the ruler. You extracted
and used her assets to build your assets,
but it was just a loan; she's coming for her
capital and interest in full.

I laughed, the world became dark and was
lit by volcanic activities while the ashes
burnt the flesh in the human lungs.
She has come to claim. We ruined her,
now it is her time for vengeance.

Human beings are viruses to her, that's her
thought, and now she will end it,
Earthquake will finish our infrastructures,
winds and water will trap and kill us.
Volcanoes will burn us to ashes; tell me,
will this be our final moment?

We built and stood on opposing sides; our
enemies are our own.
But when it's a worldwide threat we put
our differences aside until we recover, we
also recover our differences.

Can you blame Mother Nature?

No, we planned our final moments and she
set the draft.
We kill each other time after time, so why
can't she end it all?
The ending moment will be horrifying;
you'll see your loved ones as a living
skeleton.
They will be dead before you; if you're not
dead already.

Mother Nature is going all out, so drop all
your hate;
drop everything before she awakens.

The Real Me

Ambitions taller than the mountains.
Ambitions far beyond the clouds.
The sky and God are my limits, eternity
will be my measurement, a black man my
inspiration.
Legacy will be my creation; my past is just a
bitter lime that I've tasted and left behind.
But it is still a drug that pumps through my
veins—a drug that's so addicting, fuelled
with accusations, degrading statements, and
scorn.

But it's in the past now?

Yes, *maybe*, but it still lingers in my mind,
something you can't forget. It's like my
grandmother use to say—
If it doesn't kill, you use it as a fuel. Now I
use my sleepless nights to write my dreams
and dream them—
planning my reality and being productive.

Time wasters are like insects waiting for a
prey, but I'll be that predator hunting at the
top,
far beyond the idleness of sponges who
want to feed on the waters of others'
productivity.
Independence is a mind-set I use to
encourage myself; innovation is a term I
drill.
Sophisticated is a word I breathe.
Success is a world I dream of and crave far
beyond any other thing because I know
where I'm coming from.

This small kid with big dreams, this single
mother working harder than the average to
sustain her son and herself–
It changes a person;
to be judged because of his stupid
decisions that scarred him permanently.
"But who's to blame?" I'd asked.
"None, but yourself," my conscience
answered.

Just like the winds in the sea, a change is
necessary, and I've made that change
because many don't know—
This is the real me.

Brother's Love

"Doctor, doctor will she be okay?" As the
time passes, she's like a burning flame.
Dying, pale, controlled by death's hand, a
face so pure, so innocent;
losing its quality, its color and its life just as
fast.
His throat blisters, his blood boiled; his
heart raced, his guilt tormented him.
A lung aiming to fracture, he fell on his
knees—his sister is dying.
Oh Lord, please! His only sister. *Oh Lord,
please.*
Icy wind that wasn't there passes, his blood
ran cold.
The thought of losing his sister was a book
he didn't want to unfold.
"Doctor, doctor what can I do?" His fear
crawled deeper, as the scene becomes real.
She just coughed; her breath became weak,
a brother's eyes burning with streams.

A doctor's face looking helpless it seemed.
But there is one hope—just one,
he was told. He took a look once again at
her little face, his heart pleading.
He was going to do it; he sighed the
decree. He lied on the bed—a last tear
shed.
He held her hand before closing his eyes.
How can someone be full of so much
love?
Yet, he's heartless?
A young little flower, in her prime lives,
and a tree withers and gave her another
chance to shine.

Angel in a Human Body

They say beauty comes from within, but
you doubled it with elegance.
The world in and out is like a painting
fixed on a wall,
an ice tossed in a flame;
such an image would be profound to say
if the flames were laid to rest,
but they kept raging because nothing
understandable
is found within beauty but insane
perception.

My Inspiration

The black solitude, empty and void, a
whisper in the ear is like an explosion in
the house.
Calm, cool and solemn, such a wonderful
feeling—it's here, this is what I've been
waiting on.
Away from the world yet I'm in the world,
how can this be.
I see the stars in near reach, fiery with
radiation and toxicity overwhelming my
imagination.
I swam the volume of water under the sea;
I rode titanic and watch that questionable
couple burn within the cold water.
All in solitude I watched the earth
consume itself. I've heard the contradictory
statements politicians made—all in this
inspirational place—
This is my inspiration, the silent midst of
the sweet and soft, the echoing of chaos

gone from what seems to be just a
moment.
Animals went to rest and the nocturnal
take their rant, focused for a while, I'll try.

A clear head,
.101 percent unlocked. Forgive me if my
calculation is wrong but I don't really care,
for this moment of peace has locked me in
its grips.

This lovely solemn, this lovely night,
reminiscing on my life and getting closer
with my inner being.
This lovely gift. While others dream,
this love poem will take its form—
This night, this world, this inspiration will
take its form.

In Me, Beauty Lies

Sought in the heavens, many have searched.
Sought in the storm, many have failed to reach.
Tired and miserable,
Desperate, it's inevitable,
Edging, it's unforgettable.
It drives you mad; it makes you crazy.
But forget it; you've searched for it for a million days–

"It's on my skin, maybe on my face,
a trophy in my jeans, oh yes, for our babes."

You want it bad, but no, you're rejected,
For the beauty you've sought–isn't on your face,
nor in your eyes, or on your lips.
For it's in you and in me.

Mind Slaves

Disaster struck, those worthless fools,
finding themselves being corrupted, the
more you have the better—isn't it true?

destruction stuck

The idols you see, who have given all for
just a few,
will be weeping like fools. Will you be one
too?
The fame, the treasures—all gone.
The wants outweigh the needs.
You want this, you want that; such a mind
is a trap.
A slave to your mind is what you are—
distasteful at that.

Social media controls your life; the artistes
set your guideline.
Where's the era that our ancestors fought
for?

Freedom—many are yet to be free.
Slaves to technology; “freedom of speech”
is only for people with power,
and you sit back and stand by—such
wickedness.
Because they’re not free thinkers.
They’re not independent.

My Tears

The last tear that ran down my face, the
last broken heart I've felt.
My last rejection—her rejection—yet I want
her more.
She's bonded by a friend's code, I respect
that, and I respect her even more.
I found the one I love but this line she
drew—I can't take a step more.
She's like an angel, her dark skin so pure.
A fizzle in my mind, I'm so confused; this
line is confusing.
Torn between my respect for her and my
desire,
tell me what to do, but I can hold on no
more.
I want you to be continuously flourishing
like the flower you are.
I know what I'm going to do,
I'll be a shadow in your life, depending on
the lighting—
I'll be as consistent as you want me to be.

Price of Living

That slight hurt you feel because of
people–
that piercing, burning tear, that ripples the
heart when you are made to feel like trash,
that moment of isolation that makes you
feel unworthy, that slight thought of suicide
that flashes across your mind,
that cigarette puff you take, inhaling,
holding, to clear your mind.
The burning alcohol that melts the back of
your throat, fighting the equally as hot
sorrow.

Oh . . .

That moment of silence

Let's reflect on life,
This moment we live in, what they call the
present, the gift, but gifts can be sometimes
bitter.

The truth—it burns
people are a disappointment.
the gift—the pain,
The bittersweet of life—is actually a gift,
yet it is a mystery.
The price of living is an affliction, but
anything that is wonderful
will have a devastating after effect.

Your Smile, My Sunshine

The petals fall in autumn, your smile falls
upon my heart.
The moon comes out at night, your
sunshine rains on my day.
Your smile is like the spring; warm like the
upcoming summer breezes.
It whispers to my soul, like the incense in
my home.
That micro-magic, that gleaming fever, that
burning interest grasps my mind,
the zeal increases daily, momentarily as I
stare.
Your beauty increases like the aurora over
the arctic—such a changing grace,
a moving feature which gravity doesn't
control.
There's only one thing I know now, and
that's your smile;
a dyer's desire to polish you to the colour
of his heart but

you are my sunshine, so to my heart's
colour you will be.

People Change

Like a Shift . . . in time, like a pea in a pot,
The movement of people sway like swans
on the river's pure waters.
It's empty like the voids of the heartless;
it's a shadow hidden in the darkness,
and the venom of the viper,
the mind of people is that wicked smile
that seems so precious but has a hidden
agenda.
People are predators, they approach slowly
and cunningly.
They pamper and mislead, they attack
when you're down.
They leave their scar–if you survive the
battle,
and turn their backs on you when you're
weak.
They appear when you're strong, once
again–such level of persistence–
to test you–now mentally,
and begin their assault.

That Sweet Touch

That touch you speak of that chill in my
words,
that gift you speak of, those magical words.
I lost them, didn't I? Yes, I did; there is no
more magic when I look in your eyes.
There's no more smile on your lips when I
try.

My heart is empty, so heavy; there are
more tears now when I cry.
I try and try but efforts go unjustified now.

That touch you speak of, the passion I
once had,
that gift you speak of, your heart I once
had.
The trust the commitment, the faith, the
grace–
all that is erased!

I cursed myself but it's what an asshole
deserves.
The good we had, that is what we gain,
what we lose,
what we bond with,
and lose ourselves when we lose it.

Just Give Me You

Such utter foolishness!
The lines I draw are strong and bold.
Don't turn back, don't play the fool,
don't be a lost wonder.
Come to me and be my whisper of air,
be my dove and my spring of water.
Fill my lungs with refreshing songs.
Press your lips against mine so I can feel
complete.
I don't want you to go;
we've gone through too much.
We have to break through this darling.
Just give me you, give me the world.
Give me you, so I may feel perfect once
again.

Mental Warfare

As both worlds collide, you struggle to
differentiate right from wrong.
Your questions know no bounds; your
feelings are in unrest.
Images of the past tear away your sanity.
Your sanity is no longer with you.

Subtle tongue, tight veins, you cursed them
by names.
You fought their war, yet these wretches
laughed,
but you were the selected of thousands
who fit this task.
"Mercy, please," you'd begged, as your
sanity slipped away.
Prayer and faith increased as your heart,
body and mind decayed.
But the rhythms thumped, as only the gods
who fought these wars came back and
made it on their way.

White walls surrounded every corner;
black doors closed every entrance.
Skin white as the winter's growth, soul as
empty as the carcass' birth.
The horrified scream of the storm raged in
your head and the endless blisters of
heated-rage danced in your spirit.
The waves spiral on the awoken seas; this
dream is all too real,
morphed into the *all too real*—your fear
crawled closer.

The silent air humbled under the heavenly
night;
a moment of silence for the tormented
mind.
Incenses burn to keep a violent soul in
keep.
The bitter fuel in the heart blinded the
eyes to the world.
A prisoner in his own sanity, a warrior in
mental warfare
is now storming into battle, running on
paper-thin ice.

Stop, take a deep breath. You hear that?
That small thump?
Hush, stay quiet for a moment, that's just your heart.
Do you still feel sane?
The world you fought to recreate, is it still under your control?
Does the path you walk end at the gates of peace?
Or is your torment still toiling?
It's time to set your mind at ease.
As you lay in that bed, covered by that white sheet,
may your mind, body and soul, rest in peace.

They say the souls of the misunderstood will rise again,
to torment the enemies of their once-living being.
As they float over the conscience of the hypocrites
and feed upon the guilt, don't close your eyes to cry for them.

The warfare enhanced in the mind of the
now-dead was far beyond what they could
bare.
So, the dead are now raving.
They are screaming,
"Await our return.
Warriors of this mental warfare,
will taste victory."

“Nigga”

A term used to degrade.
When was it wrong to be born with a colour?
When was it right to discriminate?
When was it right to class people by group?
Aren’t we all flesh and blood?

The word used to degrade our ancestors are now being slipped into our daily conversation.

No! You can’t class me like that.
That’s the white man’s speech!

I have emancipated myself far beyond that now. I am independent! I am a ‘Sir,’ ‘A mister,’
a well-rounded individual, not a slave man!

I have a skin of rich history, a skin filled
with power,
a skin of *identity*, a skin of *determination.*

My skin is not corrupt; you say that
because your minds are filled with iniquity
and are bitter—so ignorant.
You fear us. Admit it.
You want to control us again. Admit it.
Because we are strong and bold,
we see through your acts.
You want to be on top,
But we are here; it hurts you to see us lead.

How is it the best of black were
assassinated
and the ones who stood up as well?
Hmm?
As it comes to thought, there are many
explanations, but the one that is most
outstanding—*we were too powerful.*

It is a theory.

We are using the word, with it's
subliminally puncturing us; to this point,
we are still called by it, by the white men,
who think nothing of it.
To him, we are still weak.
To him, he is thinking we are still
uneducated.
I will not stand for it.
No! I say, I will not be identified as a
"nigga," but by my intellect. I'm intelligent
enough to say, "No!"
I'm a proud black and this modern-day
slavery will not hold me back.

It is rumoured

Words are scattered like the sea waves.

It is rumoured.

They spread like viruses,
and seeped into the minds of all who came
in contact.
The lies behind the truth;
the deceit behind the lies.

It is rumoured.

The ones who spread the lies and the ones
who tell you the lies,
are they not the same ones, who look you
in the eyes and say they heard lies
spreading about you?

It is rumoured.

That she is worth this price.

It is rumoured.

That he is the father.
But all these are rumours.
The thinking brain sees these as
speculations,
as *words* that want to devour the reputation
of others.

It is rumoured that he has this,
that she has that.
But the intellectual mind dismisses traded
opinions–
dismissing statements that are rumoured.

Two-Faced

They come to you all innocent and sweet,
telling you words you long to hear.
They fill your mind with their deceit, lies
and folly,
slowly taking over your mind,
controlling you like a puppet on a string.

You fall victim to the face on the outside
and know not of the one inside.
They bind your heart with chains, taking
you prisoner to your own insolence.
They make their way into your life; getting
close to your friends and family.

They watch you and make preparations for
you.
In the slightest instance where you falter,
they take advantage of the situation and
show their true colours.
Then, when you truly regret,
it's too late to turn back.

You are already a prisoner;
a prisoner of what dwells on the outside.

They cast a soothing spell,
hiding themselves once again, easing your paranoia.
So, you deduce who you are dealing with—
the *who.*

Alludes

Allude, nothing seems the same, nothing
feels the same.
Trees without roots lie covered in
medicine and injected into the head.
We talk in codes; nothing is explained.
Love– a character which alludes many. . .

Grab a glass, take a sip, taste the wine on
your tongue,
you confused fool.
Brighten your smile, look in my eyes, take
another drink.
As I lure you in the pool,
how is the water? Is it the right
temperature? Are you relaxed?
How's my hands on your thighs?
How's the bed? Is the candle just right?
You're so soft;
grant me a wish won't you. . .
give me the keys to your heart.

Do you feel the deception—a deception so
beautiful?
Why's that confused look on your face?
Didn't I give you what you've always
wanted?
Didn't I give you the love you wanted to
feel?
Allow me to strive in freedom,
that is what I want—
Grant me this freedom while I hold on to
the keys of your heart.
Both wishes are granted but alludes are
unfinished puzzles—
the pieces hidden completes the story.

Mortuus Amor...

You sat there on the throne I bestowed
upon you.
I worshipped you, praised you with crystal
tears in my eyes,
a love so strong, so soft, broke like a glass.
It was like that; my eyes opened.
Now when I look at you,
I feel the hate boiling from all the lies and
the treachery.

So, hide your face in your hands.
Kill yourself with your tears.
No one loves you, not anymore.
I was always by your side and this is how
you repay me?
I was by you all these years, and you turned
your back on me?

A sickening disgrace you have become, a
complete shell of disgust.
In this heart which now bleed black blood,

your scream is only fuel which drives this
body.
Enraged with hate you turned an Angel
into a featherless being,
and now with these shed wings, you'll crawl
on your knees and bow to your own
cruelty.

Do you know how it feels to be impaled
with lies?
Your self-righteousness is wearing thin;
listen to your best friend's lies.
She will join you with your sacrifice; she
will help you bite the hand which fed you.
I will be there though as the vultures circle
and feed upon your flesh,
and while I'm there spiting on your grave,
I'll drop a rose and whisper "*Mortuus
Amor.*"

Flesh

"Pure...Satisfaction," I stammer in your
presence.
It's a night to remember; we were not
saints.
A candlelit room, dim, it sets the mood;
a fiery body, it needed to be cooled.

A pretty British body laid on the carpet.
I poured the wine and scatter the petals.
Close your eyes and let me take control . . .

A single stroke unlocked your sensations.
The first kiss, I felt you tremble;
the first touch, I heard you moan.
Are your senses going crazy?
You're already wet;
my hands glide down your privates.
A simple touch, you blushed.
You denied the touch at first but shivered–
your body loved it.

I exhaled on your skin, and I sucked your
stiff nipples;
breasts so clean, you're skin so pure.
I felt your nails in my skin but that wasn't
enough.
Take off your panties and let's begin. . .

Your voice crumbled when I entered.
Body shivering, I knew you loved it.
Your nails entered my flesh, but the pain
was beautiful.
You called my name; it sounds broken
though.
When the tension is building, just grab my
flesh and whisper.
Tell me you love it. *Shh,* you don't have to,
your face says it all.
Bite your lips and lick them; I'll thrust it a
little harder.
This immense bliss, this sweet *sin*
is such a flawless sensation.

Temptation

I entered his chamber; I listened to his voice,

a bitter-sweet, as his lies wrapped me in a coil.

His promises stung and I looked him in the eyes.

The temptation began and I unfold my replies.

He said...

Where is your God in your struggles? The frightful days you wondered into the slums of life?

Where is your God when your mother cries? The struggles of life drag you into the gutters?
Where is your God when you are hurt and alone?

Give me your soul and let your troubles
melt away like frost on your icy window
and see the world clearly.
Money, women and smiles, intoxicate
yourself with pampered luxury and
pleasure.
Enjoy the sweet sin and the warmth of
women's love.
Watch all your enemies melt away, all the
pain of life numbed.
All you have to do is give in.
I can give you what your God hesitates to
give you.
I can tear down the obstacles and open a
new path.
I can give you the gold-lined roads and the
honeyed apples.
I can give you *Life.*

His words—fine as gold, this proposal sweet
as lime,
I replied...

Where is God? He is omnipresent? You

were there through your representatives,
right?
All the pain I go through is the drug I am
willing to take to go forward.
The gold you're willing to give is washed—
it will fade away.
The only asset I have that will be in this life
and the one beyond, why do you want it
so?
My mother cries because of the pain you
caused.

My obstacles I will pass alone—I'm willing
to take the challenges.
The love women are willing to give, I will
find the one and her love will feel like a
million.
What comes easy will fade away quickly,
and God isn't hesitant, He is patient.

Bloody Mary

I travelled through the darkness, I heard a
troubled cry.
I walked, I stumbled, I saw, I was
frightened.
What I saw was troubling, a bloodstained
virgin, heartbroken with streaks of blood
upon her cheeks.
She turned to me and spoke, "Have you
ever heard a nightmare?
Let me tell you mine."

Have you ever loved a liar, with lies that
forced you under a sheet?
Have you ever loved someone whom
you're willing to give your heart for
and that person accepted it, held it with
care and behind your back tossed it aside
like a tasteless fruit?
You feel so heartbroken, that it feels like
your entire body was crushed by a boulder.

Fuck

Her tears were felt from where I was standing;
I felt the fever in my eyes.

It's like that person was the only thing keeping you from your insanity;
that person was the voice keeping you from jumping off the ledge;
that person was the yin and you were the yang;
that person was the carbon dioxide killing the flames that wanted to consume you.

Then, on that day, his special day, you opened the door.
Then the truth opened your eyes.
That person sharing the love gave you to an unknown.
She moaned like the little whore she was,
and *he* was there taking in the moment.

But tonight, as he lied there so innocent with a smile on his face,
I leaned over and kissed his lips. He

opened his eyes;
this cold steel knife stung his heart, his pain
was my joy;
his blood covered my body. I guess this
was physical love.
He was a bitch, and now, he cursed me.
As he looked into my eyes, he smiled,
and on his dying, lying lips, he whispered,
"I love you."

I stood there... What should I do?
She gave me the knife,
and bore her chest.

What should I do!?
"Kill Me!"

Eagle's Ink

(Letter to My Woman)

Madam, how far away you are.
I traveled over this *woman* so deep she has colored my brain.
Her waves have made me sick but I still manage to remember her smile perfectly.
Madam, where art thou?
This eagle has soared the skies searching for thee.
My lungs are scarred from the journey.
This ink on these papers are rotten from the journey.
Madam, will you allow this rose to lose its petal. Will you turn up, Madam?
My hands are scarred from this journey; my flesh is bare. I've climbed mountains for thee.
The ink on this paper is my blood.
Madam, do you truly care?
Madam, are you truly fair?
Oh, how I long to see you smile, Madam.

Was that kiss one of truth or was it a
goodbye truly?
Do you truly love me Madam or is this
infatuation?
Madam, I don't know your name,
but I know your face.
Madam, I will not stop writing until I see
your face once again.
Madam.

Mother

As I'm about to read this,

I reflect upon the times I neglected to think
about the good you've done.
I reflect upon the times I forgot to tell you
I loved you.
I reflect upon the times we argued and I
said something I now regret.
I reflect upon the lies I've told you.
But what I want to tell you is...

Mother, you're such a beauty.
You're strong, you're brave and you are
magnificent.
You've taught me so much when I knew so
little.
You brought me back to health when I was
so weak.
You pulled through the tight slips and
manage to come out on top so many times,
and through all that, you maintained your
independence.

Mother, you're a warrior and I'm blessed
to have you.
Words cannot express my gratitude.
Although I may not be the perfect child,
and
the relationship we have is not so perfect
either,
you are an imperfectly-perfect mother.
Many wish to have a mother like you.
Many wish they had a mother.
Many had a mother and didn't get to tell
her that they loved her.
Many told her that they loved her when
she had passed.
But now that I have the chance,
now that I have the breath and you have it
too,
I want to say, I love you.

Winter

Dying in the ease of the shift
a frame of darken husk,
no petals to show life.
I watch in my empty shed,
isolated on that hill.
No one comes to play;
your coat has gone.
Nothing is left
but
the storm,
then life.

Russian Roulette

You are worthless!
Load your gun, place it to your ears.
You are nothing!
Feed your head with another lie.
The gun is getting heavy,
pass it on.
Now you are worthless.
Pull the trigger.
This is now light as a feather;
your chest is hot as a fever.
Feed your ears once again;
feed your temper.
Squeeze the trigger,
lie in your endeavor, because you'll place
the gun,
once more
and kill yourself with your lies.

Empty

My heart is empty as a grave;
my penalty black as the coffin.
When I am empty, I hear no sound.
The forest of life has no more life;
the winter's syntax has no more love.
Tell me what I'm doing wrong.
Tell me oh someone,
why—why do I feel nothing?
Everyone has gone.
No, has left.
No more life.
No more whispers.

Floating in this vast sea of darkness,
the eagle flocks towards the sun,
as it's the only source of light.
As it devours, so does my hope.
For the only source of light
is the only source of destruction,
and as this black ink drips on this page,
the message conceived in your mind,
is emptiness. . .

Sin

Roses are red, violets are blue,
this black rain that falls on me
is as thick as dew,
and it washes my soul.
Black as leaves little space for blue.

I'm so confused..

Greed,
lust,
defiance,
has trapped me in this vice.
Hope,
repentance,
purity,
melts on the surface of my skin.

Who am I again?

When the angel sing, my ears are plugged;
when the demons screech, I hear.
When my father speaks,
I feel guilty.
When the diamond glimmer,
my eyes turn gold.

Am I a shell of dust now?
Am I?

Can someone save me?

My eyes bleed as I look to the skies.
My body becomes numb,
my heart becomes silent
and my body becomes dust.
Just as I feared, my riches will stay.
Now I am gone. . .
because the wages of sin *is Death.*

Glass Eater

The words they choke on are the poison
they fed themselves.
Who's to blame them?
I was born a failure—I was born a sinner,
but the world gave me posture,
this mountain gave me a horizon,
and the sun gave me a gold lining.
The storm gave me lightning.
The lightning struck the sand;
it gave me glass,
I gave it
to you.
My failures
aren't just failures;
they are my staircase,
my trials, my tribulations.
So, when I'm judged as a failure,
and the storm is blowing,
I look in the mirror and I see a mountain,
then I remove the poisons you tried to feed
me,

and I watch you later below me,
eating the poison I removed.

Message from the Author

To my page turners, I want to thank you for consuming the words I bled into these pages and for making it thus far. I also thank you in advance for sharing my art piece with your friends and family members.

If you wish to connect with me, follow me:
@chensonabennett on Instagram or
@chensonbennett on Twitter

A publication by Tamarind Hill Press
www.tamarindhillpress.co.uk

TAMARiND HiLL
.PRESS

Lightning Source UK Ltd.
Milton Keynes UK
UKHW010704060920
369433UK00001B/4

9 781647 864293